DECONSTRUCTING POWERF[

MW00903922

JAMES
BALDWIN

CAMBRIDGE DEBATE SPEECH

REBECCA SJONGER

CRABTREE
PUBLISHING COMPANY
WWW.CRABTREEBOOKS.COM

CRABTREE
PUBLISHING COMPANY
WWW.CRABTREEBOOKS.COM

Author:
Rebecca Sjonger
Series research and development:
Janine Deschenes and Ellen Rodger
Editorial director:
Kathy Middleton
Editor:
Ellen Rodger
Proofreader:
Wendy Scavuzzo
Graphic design:
Katherine Berti
Image research:
Rebecca Sjonger and Katherine Berti
Print and production coordinator:
Katherine Berti

Images:
Alamy Stock Photo
    ClassicStock: p. 21 (bottom)
    Science History Images: p. 26
Associated Press, Bill Hudson: p. 28–29
Getty Images
    Anthony Barboza: p. 7 (top right)
    Bettmann: p. 33, 36
    Justin Sullivan/Staff: p. 37
    Keystone/Stringer: p. 10
    Peter Dunne: p. 9 (top right), 17
    Steve Schapiro: p. 7 (top left), 30
    Tibrina Hobson: p. 31 (top left)
    Underwood Archives: p. 38
Library of Congress: p. 19
    Pettus, Peter: p. 11 (top)
    Stearns, Junius Brutus, 1810–1885,
        artist: p. 18
Shutterstock, a katz: p. 43 (bottom)
    Cvandyke: p. 42
    eddtoro: p. 36
    Everett Historical: p. 25
    Video Pow Wow: p. 41 (top)
Smithsonian National Museum of
    African American History &
    Culture: p. 39 (books bottom
    left and bottom right)
Gift of the Baldwin Family: p. 39
    (Playbill bottom center)
University of California Berkeley Library
    Sponsored by the Cambridge Union
    Society, http://oskicat.berkeley.edu/
    record=b22146014~S1, Screen

Shot 2018-10-19 at 12.15.07 PM:
    p. 8 (video inset)
www.lib.berkeley.edu, Screen Shot
    2018-10-19 at 12.28.26 PM:
    p. 11 (inset bottom right)
Wikimedia Commons
    © 1971 ABC Television: p. 22
    Allan Warren: p. 1, 3, 9 (top left)
    Bart Everson: p. 41 (bottom)
    Cecil Stoughton, White House Press
        Office (WHPO): p. 6
    Daniel Salomons: p. 39 (top)
    Getty Center, Henry P. Moore: p. 27
    Library of Congress. Flagg, James
        Montgomery, 1877–1960, artist:
        p. 35
    Library of Congress. New York
        World-Telegram & Sun
        Collection. Dick DeMarsico,
        World Telegram staff
        photographer: p. 24
    L. Prang & Co. print of the painting
        "Hancock at Gettysburg" by Thure
        de Thulstrup, showing Pickett's
        Charge. Restoration by Adam
        Cuerden: p. 20–21 (top)
    Om285: p. 5, 9 (bottom left)
    Rob Croes, Anefo: front cover, p. 15
    SPC 5 Bert Goulait, US Military:
        p. 31 (bottom right)
    Waud, Alfred R. (Alfred Rudolph),
        1828–1891, artist: p. 23
All other images by Shutterstock

Library and Archives Canada Cataloguing in Publication

Sjonger, Rebecca, author
        James Baldwin : Cambridge debate speech /
Rebecca Sjonger.

(Deconstructing powerful speeches)
Includes bibliographical references and index.
Issued in print and electronic formats.
ISBN 978-0-7787-5239-4 (hardcover).--
ISBN 978-0-7787-5254-7 (softcover).--ISBN 978-1-4271-2183-7 (HTML)

        1. Baldwin, James, 1924-1987--Juvenile literature. 2. Speeches,
addresses, etc., American--African American authors--Juvenile literature.
3. Debates and debating--United States--History--20th century--Juvenile
literature. 4. United States--Race relations--Juvenile literature. 5. Race
discrimination--United States--Juvenile literature. 6. Blacks--United States--
Social conditions--Juvenile literature. 7. African Americans--United States--
Social conditions--Juvenile literature. 8. Civil rights--United States--Juvenile
literature. I. Title.

PS3552.A45Z893 2019   j818'.5409   C2018-905559-6
                                                                    C2018-905560-X

Library of Congress Cataloging-in-Publication Data

Names: Sjonger, Rebecca, author.
Title: James Baldwin : Cambridge debate speech /
    Rebecca Sjonger.
Description: New York, New York : Crabtree Publishing Company, [2019] |
    Series: Deconstructing Powerful Speeches |
    Includes bibliographical references and index.
Identifiers: LCCN 2018050341 (print) | LCCN 2018054548 (ebook) |
    ISBN 9781427121837 (Electronic) | ISBN 9780778752394 |
    ISBN 9780778752394 (hardcover :alk. paper) |
    ISBN 9780778752547 (paperback :alk. paper)
Subjects: LCSH: Baldwin, James, 1924-1987--Oratory--Juvenile literature.
Classification: LCC PS3552.A45 (ebook) |
    LCC PS3552.A45 Z886 2019 (print) | DDC 814/.54--dc23
LC record available at https://lccn.loc.gov/2018050341

Crabtree Publishing Company

www.crabtreebooks.com   1-800-387-7650

Printed in the U.S.A./012019/CG20181123

**Published
in Canada
Crabtree Publishing**
616 Welland Ave.
St. Catharines, Ontario
L2M 5V6

**Published in the
United States
Crabtree Publishing**
PMB 59051
350 Fifth Avenue, 59th Floor
New York, New York 10118

**Published in the
United Kingdom
Crabtree Publishing**
Maritime House
Basin Road North, Hove
BN41 1WR

**Published
in Australia
Crabtree Publishing**
3 Charles Street
Coburg North
VIC 3058

CONTENTS

INTRODUCTION

More than 700 people packed into the Cambridge Union Society on February 18, 1965. Most of them were students at the University of Cambridge in England. A television crew filmed the audience in the great hall. Host Norman St. John-Stevas was **astonished**. "I don't think I've ever seen the Union so well attended," he said. "They're on the benches, they're on the floor, they're in the galleries, and there are a lot more outside clamoring to get in."

University of Cambridge, United Kingdom

Debating is a tradition at the Cambridge Union Society hall.

The Cambridge Union was the world's oldest **debate** club. In a debate, at least two speakers present opposing views on a motion. This is a statement or question about a subject. The club's members and guests had shared lively exchanges of ideas for 150 years. To celebrate its big anniversary, people from around the world were invited to speak. They were often experts from their fields. The debates focused on issues that were important at the time.

TIMELINE

1865	Slavery is made illegal in the United States
1870	African American men gain the right to vote
1924	August 2, James Baldwin born
1957	Baldwin meets Martin Luther King Jr. and joins **civil rights movement**
1964	Civil Rights Act becomes law
1965	February 18, Baldwin–Buckley debate at Cambridge
1965	Voting Rights Act becomes law
1987	Baldwin dies in France

DEBATING A DREAM

That night's event came at a time of conflict in the United States. The country was struggling with racism. In 1964, the Civil Rights Act had become law. The act made it illegal to **discriminate** against people. They could not be treated unfairly based on things such as skin color. The new law was a good start, but true equality for all still did not exist.

At the time, many African Americans were fighting for their share of the American dream. This is the belief that every citizen can succeed if they work hard. The motion that drew such a large crowd at the Cambridge Union was: "The American dream is at the expense of the American negro." (The term "negro" was often used at the time. Most people now find it offensive.)

The audience was mainly young white British men. They clapped loudly as Peter Fullerton, the president of the club, arrived. He wore a tuxedo with a white bow tie. In fact, everyone there was dressed up. This was common for Union debates in that era. The speakers followed Fullerton to their places in the hall. They sat by wooden podiums on which they could place their notes.

The club's tradition was to have students present the main debaters. David Heycock stood up first. He introduced William F. Buckley Jr.

Civil rights leader Martin Luther King Jr. looked on as President Lyndon Johnson signed the Civil Rights Act in 1964.

Some viewers noted that William F. Buckley Jr. almost looked bored as James Baldwin spoke.

The FBI monitored James Baldwin because of his fight for African Americans' rights.

Buckley was the editor of a newspaper called *The National Review*. Heycock described him as a well-spoken **conservative**. Next, Heycock introduced James Baldwin. He was a famous writer and supporter of the American civil rights movement. Since the mid-1950s, Baldwin and other African Americans had fought for equal opportunities in voting, schools, jobs, and many other areas of life.

After Heycock introduced the debaters, he outlined the argument in favor of the motion. He described "a society which above all values freedom and equality" but where "one man in nine has been denied those rights which the rest of that society takes for granted." Fullerton then invited the next student, Jeremy Burford, to describe the

opposing argument. Burford made it clear that his side was against the motion—not against African Americans or civil rights. Studying and presenting arguments on ideas a person may not personally agree with is a part of debating.

The **anticipation** for the main debaters was building. Finally, the club's president called up James Baldwin. The eager audience began to applaud again. Baldwin had 15 minutes to convince them that the motion was true. He would argue that African Americans paid the price so that others could have the American dream. Then William F. Buckley Jr. would have the same amount of time to argue that this was not the case. St. John-Stevas claimed it "could prove one of the most exciting debates" in the history of the Union.

CHAPTER 1

PERSUASIVE PRIMARY SOURCES

The speech that James Baldwin gave in his debate with William F. Buckley Jr. is a primary source. It is an original, firsthand account of American life in 1965. Baldwin describes the experiences of many African Americans at the time. We can also learn about the civil rights movement in the 1950s and 1960s from his speech. Other kinds of primary sources include texts, audio, and images. For example, the film of the debate and photos of it are primary sources. So is recorded data. This includes the results of the vote to decide who won the debate.

A DEEPER LOOK

Secondary sources use materials from primary sources. They may be created well after an event or era took place. These sources offer a kind of explanation called an interpretation. They also give context, which is background information. Using more than one primary source allows them to present a wider point of view. Often, secondary sources analyze or give an opinion about something. School textbooks, magazine articles, and documentary films are all examples of secondary sources.

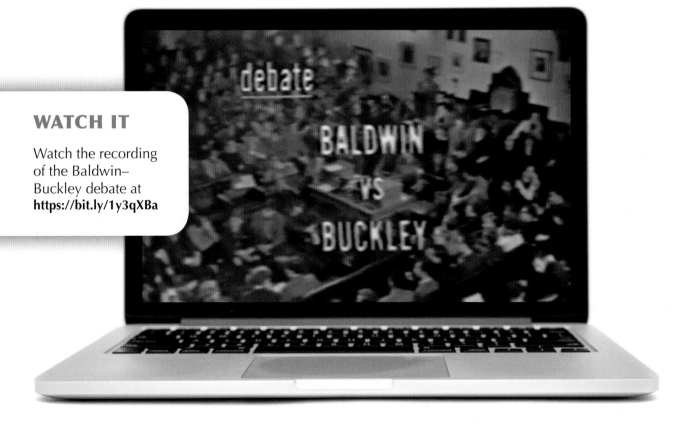

WATCH IT

Watch the recording of the Baldwin–Buckley debate at **https://bit.ly/1y3qXBa**

FACT FINDING

Finding a few basic facts is the first step in analyzing a primary source. To get started, research the following. Get as much information as possible!

Maker, such as a writer

Intended audience

Date it was created

FEBRUARY 18, 1965

Purpose

Place it was delivered

Maker's point of view

CAMBRIDGE DEBATE DETAILS

The National Educational Television network filmed the debate at Cambridge in 1965. As the crowd waited with anticipation, the network's narrator identified the location and the audience, then Norman St. John-Stevas took over:

> *This debate was held recently at the Cambridge Union, Cambridge University, England...Here we are in the debating hall of the Cambridge Union. Hundreds of undergraduates and myself waiting...*

Norman St. John-Stevas, the host of the televised debate, was president of the Union when he was a student at Cambridge.

Cambridge student David Heycock supplied other key details. He introduced James Baldwin as one of multiple speechmakers shown in the recording. Heycock also spoke about events that took place at the beginning of February 1965. This makes it clear that the debate took place at the end of that month. His overview supplied the purpose of Baldwin's speech, too.

> *Mr. James Baldwin is hardly in need of introduction. His reputation both as a novelist and as an advocate of civil rights is international...A few weeks ago, Martin Luther King had to hold a **non-violent demonstration** in Selma, Alabama...[I] propose the motion that the American dream is at the expense of the American negro...*

DIGGING DEEPER

Some primary sources from the past use terms that are now seen as offensive. Do you think these words should be changed for today's audiences? Why or why not?

A protest against rules that blocked African Americans from voting

Arguing this was Baldwin's purpose, as well as his own point of view

In 1965, the world watched as protesters called for equal rights for African Americans.

CHECK THE FILES

Some primary sources do not include all the details needed to analyze them. The video of the Baldwin–Buckley debate does not state the specific date, for example. If this information is known, it may be found in databases known as catalogs. Libraries and other organizations collect and enter data about their sources in these catalogs. The public can then search them. To find the date of the debate, the first stop might be checking the records at the Cambridge Union Society.

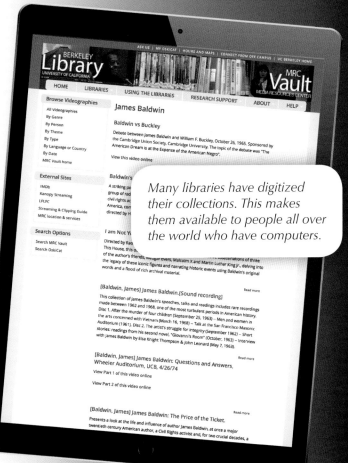

Many libraries have digitized their collections. This makes them available to people all over the world who have computers.

A POWERFUL TOOL

Speeches usually focus on an issue from one point of view. A speaker's goal is often to push for change. Words are used carefully to gain the support of the audience. Some of the most common features found in persuasive speeches are described below.

MAKING AN ARGUMENT

CLAIM

Speeches support their arguments with claims, which are statements or conclusions.

All students should wear a school uniform.

WARRANT

Warrants connect claims and evidence to support a course of action.

Students should wear uniforms to make being at school better for everyone.

EVIDENCE

Evidence is data or facts that prove the claims are true.

Students feel a greater sense of belonging when everyone wears the same uniform.

APPEAL

Appeals in speeches urge the audience to act.

If you want students to have the best experience at school, get them into uniforms!

INFLUENCING THE AUDIENCE

Rhetoric is the art of **persuasion** used in speeches and many other texts. Rhetorical language convinces the audience using three main strategies.

LOGOS

Logos urges the audience to apply logic, or reason. In a speech, logos may start with facts, then draw conclusions. It could also begin with a claim that is backed by facts.

Many schools with uniforms report less bullying. Making students feel safe in their classes is more important than individual fashion choices.

ETHOS

Ethos relies on the speaker's good character. The audience may be swayed by sharing personal experiences, finding common ground, or showing respect.

As a teacher, I respect parents' rights to choose what their kids' wear. My own child wears a uniform. I support it because I know they help students have a better time at school.

PATHOS

Pathos wins over an audience by playing on their emotions.

When students wear the same uniform, it makes it easier to spot strangers who do not belong in the school. It is a safety issue!

Whether students should wear uniforms is a popular debate motion.

LOGOS • ETHOS • PATHOS

WORDS THAT WORK

Rhetorical devices are helpful ways to boost rhetorical language. These tools include:

- Using figurative language, such as **metaphors** and **similes**
- Comparing two things that are not alike in an **analogy**
- Repeating key words and phrases
- Exaggerating in **hyperboles**
- Giving animals, objects or ideas human qualities through **personification**
- Making some facts sound less important than they really are

Writers of speeches take great care to choose just the right words to make an argument.

HEARD NOT READ

Silently reading the text of a speech is not the same experience as hearing it delivered out loud. Speechmakers think about how the words will affect their audiences. They change their language to help them win their arguments. In addition, words can be presented differently depending on how the speakers use their voice. They could alter their diction, for example. This is how a speaker pronounces and produces the sounds in words. Diction also includes the words used. Changing the tone in which words are said can add emphasis or change the message. Cadence is the rising and falling rhythms of those tones. Each of these things helps speakers reach their audiences.

FAMILY INFLUENCE

James Baldwin's stepfather, David, was a Christian **pastor**. Baldwin followed his example and became a youth minister at the age of 14. He spoke at a church in Harlem, a New York City neighborhood. Baldwin practiced using **persuasive** language and voice there for about three years. He learned to speak with confidence. Baldwin's dramatic cadence was formed during this time. This experience also influenced his writing style. He used images and characters from the Bible in his work, including the Cambridge debate. At the start of his speech, he described himself as being in the "position of a kind of Jeremiah." Jeremiah was a prophet, or someone who speaks on behalf of God. This set up Baldwin as someone the audience could trust.

James Baldwin at a book signing for the German language edition of his novel If Beale Street Could Talk.

DIGGING DEEPER

Speakers try to fit in with the setting and their audience. How would you talk to the principal if you were in trouble at school? Would you talk differently when hanging out with your friends? What might change?

CHAPTER 2

WORDS AND MEANING

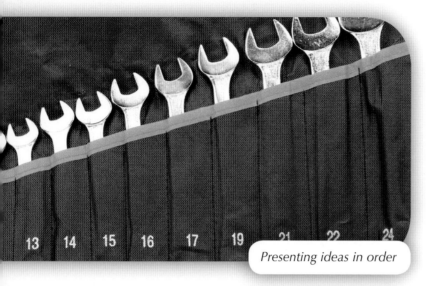

Presenting ideas in order

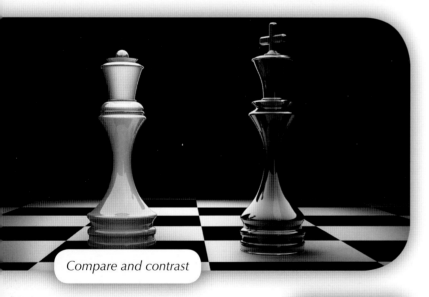

Compare and contrast

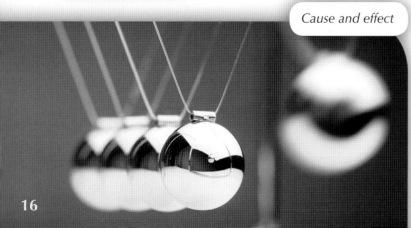

Cause and effect

Analyzing a speech is a process of deconstructing, or taking apart, each piece and looking for **intended** and unintended meaning. Once the basic details are found, the next step is to look for persuasive features and rhetorical language. Studying them shows how the speaker felt about the issue. James Baldwin focused on the central idea that people's views of the world are shaped by their experiences. His passion for the subject is revealed throughout his speech.

PRESENTING IDEAS

There are a few ways to present ideas. Placing them in order, especially when listing events, is called sequencing. Using comparison and contrast in an argument is called **comparative** style. For example, Baldwin's speech compares the experiences of African Americans and white Americans. Arranging information in a causal way means showing causes and effects. Baldwin uses all of these methods in his speech.

PURPOSE

The purpose of a speech is the reason for making it. James Baldwin's goal was to convince the members of the debating society that his side of the motion was correct. It was assigned to him for the debate. However, he agreed with it personally too.

DECONSTRUCT IT

To determine the purpose of a speech, listen to it or read it and ask:
- What is the speaker's central argument?
- Who is the speaker trying to appeal to?

Speaker: James Baldwin
Audience: The Cambridge Union
Date: February 18, 1965

> *It would seem to me that the proposition before the house, and I put it that way, is the American dream at the expense of the American negro—or the American dream is at the expense of the American negro…one's reaction to that question has to depend on…where you find yourself in the world, what your sense of reality is…*

Baldwin

The motion debated at the Cambridge Union that night

Motions may also be worded as questions

Baldwin turned the question into a conclusion to add emphasis

Factors such as race, wealth, or gender

Beliefs about racism and equality in the United States were shaped by personal experiences

In the 1960s, the members of the Cambridge Union were mostly white men.

SPEAKER SPOTLIGHT

In 1961, James Baldwin spoke at Hofstra College on Long Island. In his remarks, Baldwin argued that the United States was doomed if it did not face the truth about its own history. He questioned the greatness of some of the country's heroes. Most of these leaders owned slaves as they formed the idea of the American dream.

Speaker: *James Baldwin*
Audience: *Students at Hofstra (College) University*
Date: *May 1961*

*To destroy…the **myth** of the **founding fathers** and discover who they really were, why they came here and what they did…The problem of the **American identity** has everything to do with **all the things that happened in this country** but never have been admitted or dealt with.*

A story told over and over again until it is taken as a truth

Leaders, such as George Washington, who helped create the United States

How people from the United States view themselves

Such as using slave labor or denying equal rights

George Washington owned slaves, as did most of the earliest American presidents.

Enslaved people were among the workers who built the White House in the late 1700s.

DIGGING DEEPER

Twelve American presidents owned slaves. Do you think it would be helpful to learn more about this in history class? Why or why not?

CLAIMS AND EVIDENCE

Speeches back their arguments with statements and facts. The audience, time period, and setting affect which claims and evidence are used. Baldwin had to persuade a well-educated audience of mostly white British men. Their age was also important. Many of them had grown up hearing about the fight for civil rights in the United States.

DECONSTRUCT IT

To find claims and evidence in a speech, ask:
- What conclusions are being made?
- Which facts or data support these statements?
- Does the speaker use voice, such as emphasis or pacing, to reinforce any text?

Speaker: *James Baldwin*
Audience: *The Cambridge Union*
Date: *February 18, 1965*

> Leaving aside...the bloody **catalog of oppression**...the most serious thing this does...is to destroy his **sense of reality**...It comes as a great shock...to discover that the **flag to which you have pledged allegiance,** along with everybody else, **has not pledged allegiance to you**...It comes as a **great shock** to discover the country...**has not...evolved any place for you**...the economy— especially of the southern states— could not...be what it has become, if they had not had, and do not still have...**cheap labor**.

The evidence included a list of ways African Americans were mistreated, including murder

Beliefs that Baldwin described as held "so deeply so as to be scarcely aware of them"

A vow of loyalty to the flag, said daily by children in public schools

The pledge claims there is "liberty and justice for all"

Repeated phrase for emphasis

African Americans were left out of the country's material successes

Wealth of a country

They started a civil war to keep slavery legal

Slavery in the past and African Americans who were underpaid for their work are both evidence that the American dream is based on inequality

The southern and northern states battled in the American Civil War from 1861 to 1865.

These students pledge allegiance to the American flag in an **integrated** school in the 1960s.

21

SPEAKER SPOTLIGHT

James Baldwin was on *The Dick Cavett Show* in 1968. He appeared on the talk show with Paul Weiss, a professor at Yale University. Weiss complained about the amount of focus being placed on race. Baldwin was familiar with the **resistance** to facing the real problem of racism in the United States. He confronted Weiss, saying:

Speaker: James Baldwin
Audience: National talk show TV audience
Date: June 13, 1968

> "...that particular *social terror*, which is not the *paranoia* of my own mind but a real social danger visible on the face of *every cop, every boss, everybody*... Now this is the evidence: You want me to make an *act of faith*, risking myself, my wife...my children on some *idealism*, which you assure me exists in America, *which I have never seen*."

That the United States is not a safe place for African Americans
Fear that is not based on reason
Referred to racist white people in positions of power; boss is also a term that historically refers to overseers on slave plantations
A term with multiple meanings: doing something to test one's personal convictions and an act of sacrifice
A noble principle but often unrealistic
Baldwin used his own experience as evidence

Baldwin made a strong argument that social terror was real and lived, and racist hate translated into an ever-present threat of harm and death for African Americans. This fear was based on fact. He also used his own experience as evidence. For anyone whose ancestors had been slaves, their "sense of reality" included a long history of white people abusing their power. The menace of "every cop, every boss, everybody" had a deep, personal meaning for them.

Dick Cavett

WARRANTS AND APPEALS

Appeals in speeches request action of some kind. Warrants are the statements that support this course of action. Baldwin connected his claims and evidence in warrants to make a plea to the American people. They were not the original audience of the debate at Cambridge. However, news of the debate reached them and they heard Baldwin's argument.

DECONSTRUCT IT

Find warrants and appeals in a speech by asking:
- Is the speaker urging the audience to act or think a certain way?
- How are claims and evidence being connected to convince them?

The 15th Amendment gave African American men the right to vote. However, not every state made it a reality.

Speaker: *James Baldwin*
Audience: *The Cambridge Union*
Date: *February 18, 1965*

" *...We have a **civil rights bill** now...but if the **amendment** was **not honored** then, I don't have any reason to believe the civil rights bill will be honored now...**If one has got to prove one's title to the land**, isn't four hundred years enough?...At least three wars?... What one begs the American people to do for all our sakes is simply to **accept our history**...* "

On July 2, 1964, President Lyndon Johnson signed an act that made it illegal to discriminate against people in public places

The 15th Amendment to the U.S. Constitution allowed African American men to vote in 1870

Some states continued to block African Americans from voting

That is, a share in the American dream

Baldwin appealed to people who were not in the audience but who were most affected by the issue

EXPANDING THE MEANING

In this excerpt, Baldwin justified his lack of belief in the United States government to fix the problem. Four hundred years of history proved it. African slaves had been in North America since they arrived with Spanish explorers in the early 1500s. The number of years also connected with the ancient **captivity** of the **Israelites** in Egypt. African

American churches often compared this Bible story to the experiences of enslaved peoples in the United States. Later in Baldwin's speech, he repeated the reference to 400 years. It highlighted his frustration over the lack of progress. Despite this fact, African American soldiers were fighting in the **Vietnam War** at the time. They had fought in every major conflict involving the United States, including both **world wars**. But, their sacrifices did not result in equality.

SPEAKER SPOTLIGHT

James Baldwin gave a warning to the United States during the Cambridge debate. If its citizens did not admit that the American dream was achieved at the expense of African Americans, there would be trouble. He spoke to a writer from *Esquire* magazine a few years later. The fight for civil rights had grown bloodier over the years. Martin Luther King Jr. had been killed two months before. The interviewer asked Baldwin, "How can we get the black people to cool it?" Baldwin replied, "It is not for us to cool it." He appealed to white Americans to admit the truth about the history of the country. He argued that the United States would not exist without African Americans.

Speaker: *James Baldwin*
Audience: *Esquire magazine readers*
Date: *July 1968*

> "...if I go under in this country—I, the black man—he goes, too...It's a matter of whether or not you want to live...All that can save you now is your confrontation with your own history...[it] has led you to this moment, and you can only begin to change yourself by looking at what you are doing..."

Cease to exist
Not just Baldwin but all African Americans
The average white American
"You" referred to white people throughout
Facing up to

Martin Luther King Jr. drew huge crowds when he spoke. Those same people mourned his death by an assassin's bullet in 1968.

DIGGING DEEPER

What are some of the issues with a white person asking how to get African Americans to "cool it"?

RHETORICAL LANGUAGE

Rhetorical language, including logos, ethos, and pathos, helps make speeches stronger. It supports the claims, evidence, appeals, and warrants. For example, Baldwin told stories to draw in the audience. This pathos built empathy, or understanding, with the Cambridge students who came from very different backgrounds. Baldwin also reasoned with the students. He used the experiences of his ancestors, or distant relatives, to gain credibility. His rhetoric showed how difficult it was for the later generations of African Americans to thrive.

DECONSTRUCT IT

To identify the rhetorical language in a speech, ask:
- How is the speaker using logic and reason to persuade the audience?
- Does the speaker's character help support the central argument?
- How is the audience being swayed by emotion?

Speaker: James Baldwin
Audience: The Cambridge Union
Date: February 18, 1965

…By the time **you** are thirty, you have been through a certain kind of **mill**. And the most serious effect of the mill you've been through is…the millions of details, twenty-four hours of every day, which spell out to you that you are a worthless human being…It's by that time that you've begun to see it happening in your daughter or your son or your niece or your nephew…nothing you have done, and as far as you can tell, **nothing you can do**, will save your son or your daughter from meeting the same disaster…this is not an overstatement, that **I** picked the cotton, and I carried it to market, and I built the railroads **under someone else's whip for nothing**. For nothing.

The average African American at the time
Mills crush and pound materials, so this imagery helped create a feeling of being crushed
Baldwin painted a picture of despair
Baldwin emphasized each instance of "I"
Enslaved peoples were beaten for any reason
The American dream was achieved—but not by African Americans who worked hard for hundreds of years building up the country

CHAPTER 3

ANALYZING PERSPECTIVES

Speeches often reveal how the maker, the audience, and society felt about an issue at a certain time in history. James Baldwin was clearly passionate about the American civil rights movement in the 1960s. He shared his own perspective, or point of view. Sometimes, a speechwriter creates a speech on behalf of the person who delivers it. The writer often uses the speaker's ideas.

DIGGING DEEPER

Do you think a speechwriter and a speaker need to share the same point of view? Why or why not?

A BOY IN HARLEM

The era when a speech is made affects its perspective. Both the maker and the audience are products of their time period and setting. James Baldwin himself said, "I come out of a certain place, a certain time, a certain history." He was born and grew up in Harlem in the 1920s and 1930s, a time when African American culture boomed in what would be known as the **Harlem Renaissance**. Many African Americans moved there from southern states to escape harsh and brutal racism. Harlem offered more opportunities and freedom, yet a lack of good jobs and housing were some of the problems they faced. Growing up in this community shaped Baldwin's point of view.

More than 1.6 million African Americans migrated north from 1910 to 1930. They came from the more rural South and settled in cities such as Harlem. Harlem offered a kind of cultural freedom not available in the South.

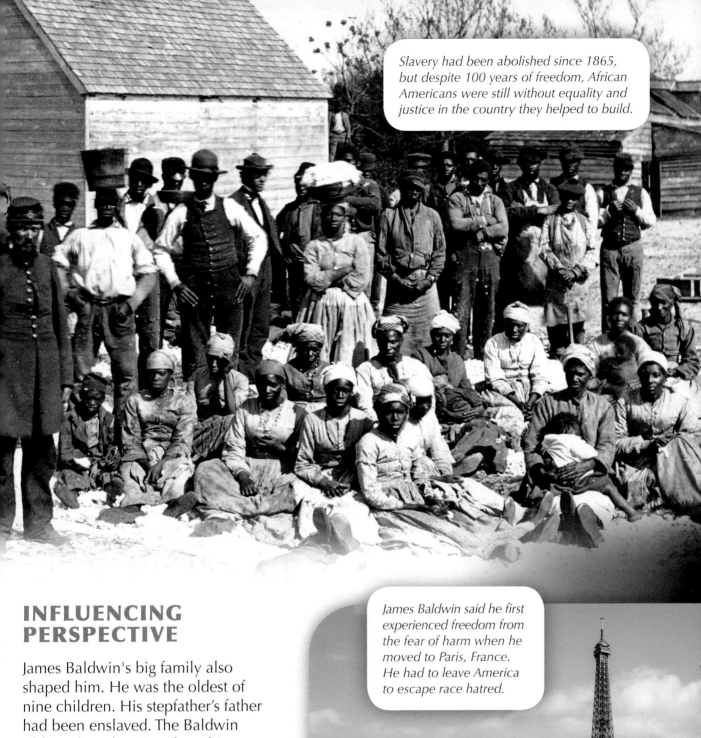

Slavery had been abolished since 1865, but despite 100 years of freedom, African Americans were still without equality and justice in the country they helped to build.

INFLUENCING PERSPECTIVE

James Baldwin's big family also shaped him. He was the oldest of nine children. His stepfather's father had been enslaved. The Baldwin siblings heard stories about his mistreatment. However, James did not hate white people. One reason was his relationship with a white teacher named Orilla "Bill" Miller. She encouraged him by giving him books and taking him to see movies and plays. This experience influenced his perspective.

James Baldwin said he first experienced freedom from the fear of harm when he moved to Paris, France. He had to leave America to escape race hatred.

DECONSTRUCT IT

To examine a speaker's perspective, ask:
- How does the language used show the speaker's feelings?
- How could the speaker's point of view be summed up in one sentence?

In the following part of Baldwin's speech, he describes his perspective. For centuries, African Americans had worked hard but they did not achieve the American dream. He warned that it was at risk if it could not be shared equally.

> *I have to speak as one of the people who've been most attacked by what we must now here call the Western or **European system of reality**…It is a terrible thing for an entire people to surrender to the **notion** that one-ninth of its population is beneath them…I am not a **ward** of America…I am one of the **people who built the country**…there is scarcely any hope for the American dream, because the people who are denied participation in it, by their very presence, will wreck it.*

Speaker: *James Baldwin*
Audience: *The Cambridge Union*
Date: *February 18, 1965*

Baldwin is referring to a system that values only white experiences

The idea

Referred to a belief held by some white people that they were superior to other races

A child, or someone who is dependent

Enslaved peoples and their descendants whose labor and accomplishments went unrecognized

The audience of the debate would have seen the clashes between police and civil rights activists in the news. This 1963 photo shows police dogs being set on a civil rights demonstrator in Birmingham, Alabama, which was the scene of many racist bombings, including one that killed four girls.

DIGGING DEEPER

Sometimes, debaters must argue something they do not personally agree with. Do you think James Baldwin's perspective could have helped him argue the opposing side of the motion? Why or why not?

SPEAKER SPOTLIGHT

In 1979, Baldwin began working on a book called *Remember This House*. It was about the lives of Martin Luther King Jr., Malcolm X, and Medgar Evers. These African American leaders each shaped the civil rights movement in their own ways. By their late 30s, each was murdered because of their beliefs. Baldwin had not finished writing the book when he died in 1987. The 2016 documentary *I Am Not Your Negro* includes text from it.

" *The story of the negro in America is the story of America. It is not a pretty story…I still believe that we can do with this country something that has not been done before…The tragedy is that most of the people who say they care about it do not care. What they care about is their safety and their profits.* "

Baldwin believed that without African Americans, the United States would not exist in its current form

Referred to the history of slavery

There was still hope in Baldwin's view

An event with an unhappy ending

Baldwin believed that most people cared more about their own American dream than making a better future for all

James Baldwin met civil rights activist Medgar Evers in January 1963. Six months later, Evers was murdered by a **white supremacist**.

WATCH IT

Clips and information about *I Am Not Your Negro* are available at **www.iamnotyournegrofilm.com**. Note that the content is rated PG-13.

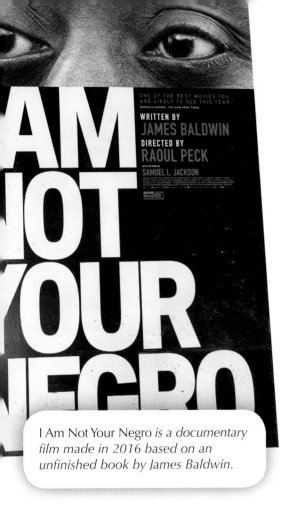

I Am Not Your Negro *is a documentary film made in 2016 based on an unfinished book by James Baldwin.*

ONE PERSON'S PERSPECTIVE

Speeches and other primary sources often present only one perspective. This limits what can be learned about an issue or time period. During a critical analysis, ask:
- How does the maker's perspective shape this primary source?
- Are any important facts being left out?
- Based on evidence from other sources, are there any points that should be explored further?

IN SOMEONE ELSE'S SHOES

James Baldwin's speech tries to look at the opposing point of view. He went so far as to try to understand white racists. Baldwin claimed that "no one can be dismissed as a total monster." He suggested that "something awful must have happened" to whites who mistreated African Americans. His perspective may have been swayed by his time living in France. "Once you find yourself in another **civilization**, you're forced to examine your own," he said.

OTHER PERSPECTIVES

Everyone has their own point of view—or sense of reality, as James Baldwin called it. The makers of primary and secondary sources have biases. This is being more or less in favor of an idea or a person. Biases can be obvious or hidden. Looking at multiple sources may reveal biases. It also leads to a fuller understanding. These materials could be from the same time period or in response to a speech. In the case of the Cambridge debate, William F. Buckley Jr. gave a direct response to Baldwin's argument. Like Baldwin, Buckley's side matched his own point of view.

SIMILAR BUT DIFFERENT

William F. Buckley Jr. was born in 1925, just a year after Baldwin. Like Baldwin, Buckley came from a large family. He was one of 10 children. They also lived in New York City. However, the Buckleys came from a much wealthier, white neighborhood. The family made their fortune in the oil business. As a boy, Buckley attended schools in France and England. Later, he graduated from Yale University in Connecticut. These experiences gave him a very different perspective than Baldwin had.

William F. Buckley Jr.

OPPOSING THE MOTION

William F. Buckley Jr. spoke as if every American understood and shared his perspective. He also argued that Baldwin's point of view as an African American did not matter. Buckley believed that anyone could follow the path to success if they worked hard enough. He admitted that racism existed but he barely addressed the ongoing fight for equal rights. There was also no response to Baldwin's argument that slaves built the country.

Speaker: *William F. Buckley Jr.*
Audience: *The Cambridge Union*
Date: *February 18, 1965*

> *…It is impossible in my judgment to deal with the indictment of Mr. Baldwin unless one is prepared to deal with him as a white man, unless one is prepared to say to him that the fact that your skin is black is utterly irrelevant to the arguments that you raise…What we need is a* **considerable amount of frankness that acknowledges that there are two sets of difficulties,** *the difficulties of the white person, brown people, and black people [who] all over the world,* **protect their own vested interests, and** *who [do] as all of the races over the entire world have and* **suffer from a kind of racial narcissism that tends always to convert every contingency in such a way as to maximize their own power…** *But* **we must also reach through to the Negro people and tell them that their best chances are in a mobile society** *and the most mobile society in the world today is in the Unted States.*

Buckley's point of view on Baldwin's claims

He states that people of different races have different world views

The belief that people will only protect their own interests

Equating striving for equality with excessive self-love and an attempt to take power

While Baldwin asks "isn't 400 years enough" and states that black people "do not belong where white people have put them," Buckley shifts the issue of racism back to those who suffer from it, while also telling them to wait longer and their country will eventually recognize them

Buckley made it sound as though Baldwin had rejected the entire American system. However, Baldwin only warned that it might be destroyed if the country did not face its failures. White Americans had to accept that they had an unearned advantage not given to black people. It prevented true equality for African Americans.

CAREFULLY CHOSEN WORDS

Word choices can reveal a speechmaker's perspective. Subtle differences in language or tone are called nuances. James Baldwin's friends Martin Luther King Jr. and Malcolm X both fought for civil rights but they had opposing points of view. King promoted nonviolent protests. Malcolm X wanted to bring about change through "any means necessary." For that reason, Malcolm X's speeches used words such as "resistance," while King was more likely to use terms such as "overcome."

Malcolm X's family was harassed by white racists when he was a child. One group even burned down his house. Here, he speaks at a civil rights rally in Harlem in 1963.

MALCOLM X'S PERSPECTIVE

Malcolm X would likely have agreed with the debate motion that the American dream is at the expense of African Americans. However, unlike James Baldwin, his perspective was that there was little hope in appealing to white Americans to act. Malcolm X thought the threat of violence was the only way to create change. In April 1964, he spoke at churches in Cleveland, Ohio, and Detroit, Michigan. These similar speeches became known as "The Ballot or the Bullet." Malcolm X urged his audience to embrace **black nationalism**. Its goal was to unite African Americans across the country.

Speaker: *Malcolm X*
Audience: *African Americans*
Date: *April 3, 1964*

> "*…We don't see any American dream. We've experienced only the American* **nightmare**…***It's liberty or it's death***. *It's freedom for everybody or freedom for nobody. America today finds* **herself** *in a unique situation…They have never had a* **bloodless revolution**… *You don't have a revolution in which you* **love your enemy**…**Revolutions destroy systems**…*So…it's the* **ballot or the bullet**…*let the world see that* **Uncle Sam** *is guilty of* **violating** *the human rights of 22 million* **Afro-Americans** *right down to the year of 1964…Don't change the white man's mind…They don't try and eliminate an* **evil** *because it's evil, or because it's illegal, or because it's immoral; they eliminate it only when it threatens their existence…*"

African Americans
Slavery in the past and unequal treatment in that time period
Quoted a famous line from a speech made by lawyer Patrick Henry in 1775; it referred to the struggle for freedom from Britain
Personification
An uprising in which there is no violence
May have referred to the perspective of Martin Luther King Jr. or teachings from the Bible
Instead of gaining equality in the current American society, Malcolm X wanted to create something new
Argued that African Americans needed to be able to vote freely or there would be violence
The United States government
Not respecting
Another term for African Americans that was common at the time
Racism that affected every part of society

Uncle Sam is a personification of the United States government.

I WANT YOU FOR U.S. ARMY

NEAREST RECRUITING STATION

CHAPTER 4

INFLUENCES THEN AND NOW

When James Baldwin was done speaking at Cambridge, the audience got to their feet. They gave him a huge round of applause. Host Norman St. John-Stevas exclaimed that he had "never seen this happen before in the Union." After Baldwin and Buckley had both argued their sides of the motion, the debating society members voted. The result was 544–164 in favor of the motion. Baldwin's persuasive speech beat Buckley's.

MALCOLM X MURDERED

A violent death a few days later helped the debate attract more attention. Malcolm X was murdered as he got ready to speak to a crowd in New York. This tragic event placed the spotlight on the civil rights movement. People around the world were watching what was happening in the United States. They wanted to learn more about the issues Baldwin was passionate about.

DIGGING DEEPER

When a newspaper prints only a portion of a speech, what limits are placed on it as a primary source?

Mourners reach out to the funeral procession of Malcolm X. He was murdered on February 21, 1965, while preparing to speak before the Organization of Afro-American Unity, a group he founded. His passionate speeches stirred many who desired respect and freedom.

SPREADING THE WORD

The New York Times printed a transcript, or written version, of the Baldwin–Buckley debate on March 7, 1965. The speeches were shortened by the newspaper. The recording was shown on television in the United Kingdom two days after the debate. It aired in the United States in June 1965. The debate summed up many people's feelings on both sides of the issue. It truly was a snapshot of the era.

Fifty years after the violence in Selma, a modern movement called Black Lives Matter marched in memory of Bloody Sunday. Modern movements, such as Black Lives Matter, continue to speak for justice and equality for all African Americans.

MOVING FORWARD

On the same day that the debate appeared in the newspaper, about 600 nonviolent civil rights protesters marched toward Montgomery, Alabama. They were attacked by the police in Selma. The clash became known as Bloody Sunday. News reports of the violence were seen around the country. Soon, there were protests across the United States. In response to the unrest, the Voting Rights Act was signed into law by President Johnson on August 6, 1965. It forced state governments to allow everyone to vote based on the 15th Amendment from the 1800s.

CHANGING WORLD

Some people kept refusing to treat other races equally. This was not surprising. It took the United States two centuries to abolish, or end, slavery. Then it took 95 years for the 15th Amendment to be put into practice so that African Americans could vote. Change was possible, but it was slow. In 1979, James Baldwin spoke to a *New York Times* journalist about his hopes.

> *In some way, your aspirations and concern for a single man in fact do begin to change the world. The world changes according to the way people see it, and if you alter, even by a millimeter, the way a person looks or people look at reality, then you can change it.*

15th Amendment

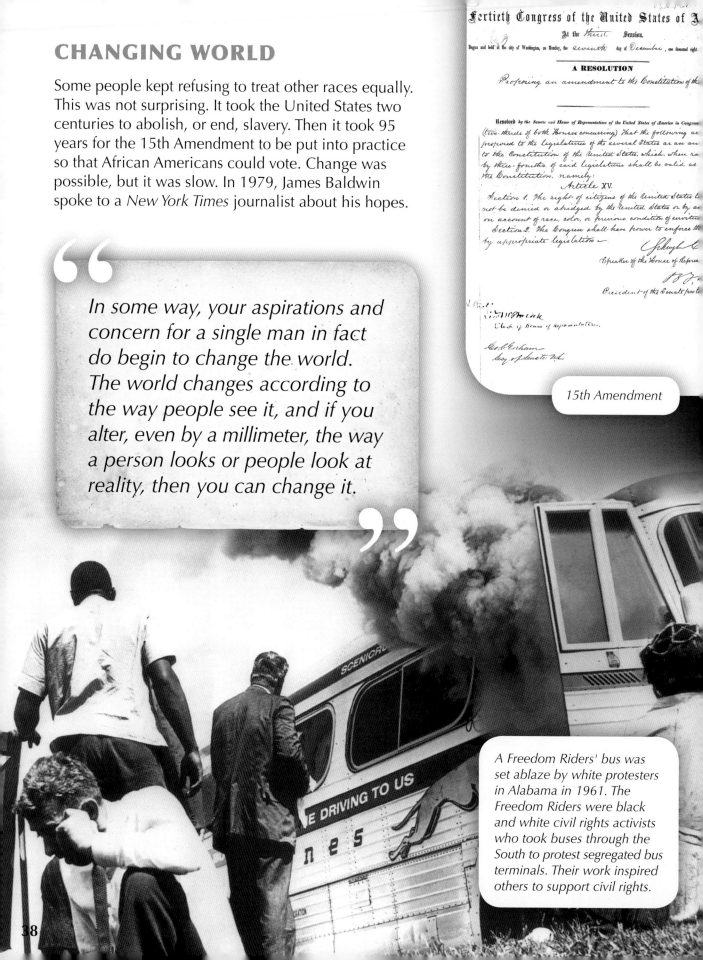

A Freedom Riders' bus was set ablaze by white protesters in Alabama in 1961. The Freedom Riders were black and white civil rights activists who took buses through the South to protest segregated bus terminals. Their work inspired others to support civil rights.

James Baldwin's house in the French village of Saint-Paul de Vence, where he wrote many of his books.

BALDWIN'S LATER LIFE

James Baldwin had already made a name for himself by the time of the debate. He continued to write books, plays, and articles. He used his celebrity to draw attention to racism and African Americans' rights. Baldwin traveled to the United States to visit his family. However, he made his home in France. In late 1987, Baldwin died there of an illness. He was 63 years old.

MODERN PERSPECTIVE

During the debate, James Baldwin asked Americans "simply to accept our history." Decades later, Mitch Landrieu was the mayor of New Orleans. He made a speech when several statues of **civil war** heroes were taken down in the city in 2017. They celebrated leaders of the **Confederate States of America**, such as Robert E. Lee and Jefferson Davis. One of the reasons these states left the **Union** in 1861 was so that they could keep slaves. He argued that it was time to face up to the nation's past and make things right, just as Baldwin had argued.

Speaker: Mitch Landrieu
Audience: New Orleans, when controversy arose over the removal of statues
Date: May 17, 2017

> ...New Orleans was America's largest **slave market**: a **port** where hundreds of thousands of souls were bought, sold and shipped up the Mississippi River to lives of forced labor, of misery...As President George W. Bush said at the dedication ceremony for the **National Museum of African American History & Culture**, 'A great nation does not hide its history. It faces its flaws and corrects them.'...These monuments purposefully celebrate a **fictional, sanitized** Confederacy; ignoring the death, ignoring the enslavement, and the terror that it actually stood for...This is...about showing the whole world that we as a city and as a people are able to... choose a better future for ourselves making straight what has been crooked and making right **what was wrong**...Centuries-old wounds are still raw because they never healed right in the first place. Here is the essential truth: we are better together than we are apart...We have to **reaffirm** our commitment to a future where each citizen is guaranteed the uniquely American gifts of **life, liberty and the pursuit of happiness**...

Place to buy people	Ships that had crossed the Atlantic Ocean arrived there
	This Smithsonian museum opened on September 24, 2016, in Washington, D.C.
	Not true and cleaned up
	Such as the American dream being achieved at the expense of African Americans
	Repeatedly strengthen
	Rights that the United States Declaration of Independence states are for all people

40

DIGGING DEEPER

There are many perspectives on removing historical statues that some people find offensive today. What are the pros and cons of leaving these statues in place?

?

Cranes remove the Robert E. Lee monument in New Orleans in 2017. The Confederate general fought for the continuation of slavery.

WATCH IT

To see Mitch Landrieu's full speech, go to **https://bit.ly/2M27T8i**

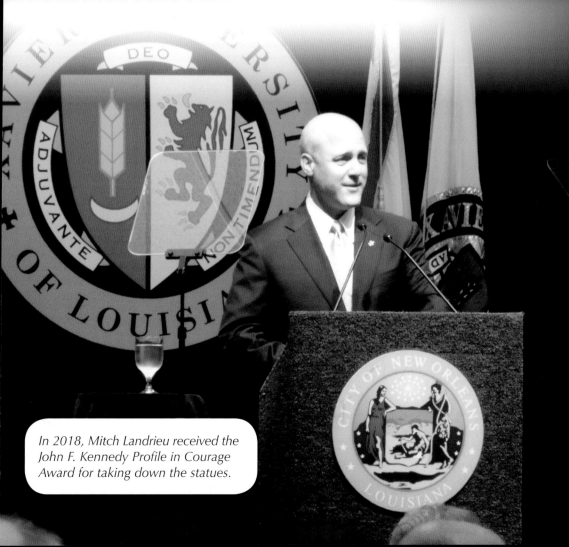

In 2018, Mitch Landrieu received the John F. Kennedy Profile in Courage Award for taking down the statues.

The National Museum of African American History & Culture has a large collection of primary and secondary sources.

LASTING SIGNIFICANCE

In 2009, someone posted a video clip of James Baldwin's speech at Cambridge. The video went viral on a variety of social media platforms. A huge audience from a new generation was exposed to Baldwin's argument. It is still relevant 40 years after the debate because American society and others around the world still struggle with racism and inequality.

THE CIVIL RIGHTS MOVEMENT IS NOT OVER

BIBLIOGRAPHY

INTRODUCTION

"1964 Civil Rights Act Fast Facts." *CNN.* https://cnn.it/2xwlgVz

Baldwin, James. "The American Dream and the American Negro," *The New York Times*, March 7, 1965.

Buccola, Nicholas. "James Baldwin, William F. Buckley Jr., and the American Dream: A Symposium," *American Political Thought, 6,(4), 2017.*

Carson, Clayborne. "American civil rights movement." Encyclopaedia Britannica, October 17, 2018. https://bit.ly/2kACitg

"Curriculum Guide: I Am Not Your Negro." Magnolia Pictures. https://bit.ly/2MTVFuz

"James Baldwin Debates William F. Buckley (1965)." YouTube, October 27, 2012. https://bit.ly/2LSlbnF

Lee, Aidan. "Baldwin v. Buckley." *BackStory.* October 9, 2016. https://bit.ly/2NY8VmN

McWilliams, Susan J., Lawrie Balfour, P.J. Brendese, et al. *A Political Companion to James Baldwin.* Lexington: University Press of Kentucky, 2017.

Sands, Leo. "50 years since historic civil rights debate at Cambridge Union." Varsity, University of Cambridge, February 18, 2015. www.varsity.co.uk/news/8295

"What Is Debating?" The Cambridge Union. https://bit.ly/29SNiCn

CHAPTER 1

Fahnestock, Jeanne. *Rhetorical Style: The Uses of Language in Persuasion.* New York: Oxford University Press, 2011.

"James Baldwin Biography." Biography, January 19, 2018. www.biography.com/people/james-baldwin-9196635

Oppenheimer, Mark. "The Downsides of School Uniforms." *The New Yorker*, September 6, 2017. https://bit.ly/2A4q7jJ

Ordway, Denise-Marie. "School uniforms: Do they really improve student achievement, behavior?" Journalist's Resource, April 20, 2018. https://bit.ly/2QQ8qd2

"Primary Sources." University of California, Irvine Libraries. www.lib.uci.edu/introduction-primary-sources

"Primary Sources: What Are They?" Teaching History. http://teachinghistory.org/best-practices/using-primary-sources/19079

"Primary vs. Secondary Sources." BMCC Library. http://lib1.bmcc.cuny.edu/help/sources

"The King Years." The King Legacy. www.thekinglegacy.org/content/king-years

"Using Primary Sources." United States Library of Congress. www.loc.gov/teachers/usingprimarysources

Weida, Stacy and Karl Stolley. "Using Rhetorical Strategies for Persuasion." Purdue Online Writing Lab. https://owl.purdue.edu/owl/general_writing/academic_writing/establishing_arguments/rhetorical_strategies.html

CHAPTER 2

"15th Amendment to the U.S. Constitution." Web Guides, The Library of Congress. https://bit.ly/1n74TQA

"African Americans in the U.S. Army." U.S. Army. https://bit.ly/2xFKfFf

Andrews, Evan. "How Many U.S. Presidents Owned Slaves?" History, July 19, 2017. https://bit.ly/2O6sd9k

Davis, Julie Hirschfeld. "Yes, Slaves Did Help Build the White House." *The New York Times*, July 26, 2016. https://nyti.ms/2zmEjmw

Guasco, Michael. "The Misguided Focus on 1619 as the Beginning of Slavery in the U.S. Damages Our Understanding of American History." *Smithsonian Magazine,* Sept. 13. 2017. https://bit.ly/2H505NP

"James Baldwin: How to Cool It." *Esquire*, August 2, 2017. https://bit.ly/2MTqGiz

Malbreaux, Tyler. "A James Baldwin Debate at 50." *The Dartmouth*, September 21, 2017. https://bit.ly/2I6lpDc

Norman, Tony. "The furious eloquence of James Baldwin." *Pittsburgh Post-Gazette*, February 17, 2017. https://bit.ly/2prU5qH

Petrella, Christopher. "The ugly history of the Pledge of Allegiance—and why it matters." *The Washington Post*, November 3, 2017. https://wapo.st/2xBbmBe

Preston, Malcolm. "The Image: Three Views— Ben Shahn, Darius Milhaud and James Baldwin Debate the Real Meaning of a Fashionable Term." *Opera News*, no. 27 (8 December 1962): 9–12.

Vaught, Seneca. "James Baldwin vs. William F. Buckley, Jr. for the Soul of America." *James Baldwin: Challenging Authors*. Springer, 2014.

Warner, John. "Why James Baldwin Beat William F. Buckley in a Debate, 540-160." Inside Higher Ed, April 8, 2012. https://bit.ly/2vmigsR

CHAPTER 3

Als, Hilton. "Capturing James Baldwin's Legacy Onscreen." *The New Yorker*, February 13 and 20, 2017. https://bit.ly/2Nud16K

Andrews, Evan. "Patrick Henry's 'Liberty or Death' Speech." History, March 22, 2015. https://bit.ly/2ppPvZD

Bellot, Gabrielle. "Baldwin vs. Buckley: A Debate We Shouldn't Need, As Important As Ever." Literary Hub, July 20, 2017. https://bit.ly/2MMWKVb

Grierson, Tim. "'I Am Not Your Negro': How a New Doc Turns James Baldwin Into a Prophet." *Rolling Stone*, February 3, 2017. https://rol.st/2OFAoXu

Jabali, Malaika. "Power in Black Politics: The Relevancy Of Malcolm X's 'Ballot Or The Bullet' Speech Today" *Essence*, May 19, 2017. https://bit.ly/2zm90IA

"James Baldwin." *Harper's Magazine*. https://harpers.org/author/jamesbaldwin

Jones, J.R. "James Baldwin: Voice of a preacher, heart of a nomad." *Chicago Reader*, February 2, 2017. https://bit.ly/2pucROj

Jones, Ryan M. "Reclaiming Malcolm X." National Civil Rights Museum, April 21, 2015. https://bit.ly/2MQ6PAx

King, Martin Luther, Jr. "'Loving Your Enemies,' Sermon Delivered at Dexter Avenue Baptist Church." The Martin Luther King, Jr. Research and

Education Institute, Stanford University. https://stanford.io/2IvtIai

"Malcolm X." American RadioWorks. https://bit.ly/2eGgDkQ

"Malcolm X Biography." Biography, January 18, 2018. https://bit.ly/2rcRTFj

Styron, William. "James Baldwin: His Voice Remembered; Jimmy in the House." *The New York Times*, December 20, 1987. https://nyti.ms/2QVycg2

"William F. Buckley Jr. Biography." Biography, August 5, 2015. https://bit.ly/2psaag3

Williams, Mason B. "Whose Harlem Is This, Anyway?" The Gotham Center for New York City History, March 31, 2016. https://bit.ly/2ps6xXh

CHAPTER 4

Black Lives Matter. https://blacklivesmatter.com

"Full speech: Mitch Landrieu addresses removal of Confederate statues." *The Washington Post*, May 31, 2017. www.youtube.com/watch?v=csMbjG0-6Ak

Holmes, Marian Smith. "The Freedom Riders, Then and Now." *Smithsonian Magazine*, February 2009. https://bit.ly/2mPxGlj

"Mitch Landrieu's Speech on the Removal of Confederate Monuments in New Orleans." *The New York Times*, May 23, 2017. https://nyti.ms/2q9ASgb

Romano, John. "James Baldwin Writing and Talking." *The New York Times*, September 23, 1979. https://nyti.ms/2xDJxlJ

"The Declaration of Independence." U.S. History. https://bit.ly/1gEm0L5

"The First March From Selma." America's Story from America's Library, The Library of Congress. https://bit.ly/2yzwWVi

"The Voting Rights Act of 1965." The United States Department of Justice. https://bit.ly/2g1d3ym

"Voting Rights Act Fast Facts." *CNN*, July 24, 2018. https://cnn.it/2AldguI

LEARNING MORE

BOOKS

Elish, Dan. *The Civil Rights Movement: Then and Now*. North Mankato: Capstone, 2018.

Henneberg, Susan. *James Baldwin: Groundbreaking Author and Civil Rights Activist*. New York: Rosen, 2015.

Roy, Jennifer Rozines. *Sharpen Your Debate and Speech Writing Skills*. New York: Enslow, 2011.

DOCUMENTARY

I Am Not Your Negro. Directed by Raoul Peck. Los Angeles: Magnolia Pictures, 2017. Film.

WEBSITES

Learn more about primary and secondary sources: **https://sccollege.edu/Library/Pages/primarysources.aspx**

Get an in-depth look at an episode about James Baldwin from PBS's American Masters: **https://to.pbs.org/1MrDh7U**

Explore American life in the 1960s through the National Civil Rights Museum's online sit-in activity: **www.civilrightsmuseum.org/standing-up**

GLOSSARY

analogy A similarity between two things from which a comparison is made

anticipation To look forward to something, or expect that it will happen

astonished To be surprised or filled with wonder

black nationalism A movement that promotes and develops black identity

captivity The condition of being confined, enslaved, or imprisoned

civil rights movement An organized effort by African Americans in the 1950s and 1960s to end legal racial discrimination and gain equal rights under the law in the United States

civil war A war between the North, or northern states, and the South, or southern states, from 1861–1865

civilization A type of society or culture that existed in a specific time and place

comparative Of or involving comparing or examining two things and noting their similarities and differences

Confederate States of America A group of (originally 7, later 11) southern states that declared their secession, or withdrawal, from the United States of America in 1861, leading to civil war

conservative Believing in the value of established and traditional practices in politics and society

debate A discussion in a public setting where two sides put forward an argument for or against an idea

discriminate To make a judgment against a person based on the group or class that a person belongs to, rather than on merit

Harlem Renaissance A period of African American cultural renewal in the 1920s and 1930s in Harlem, New York City

hyperbole Obvious and intentional exaggeration

integrated Bringing together different groups or races

intended Designed or meant for a particular reason or purpose

Israelites A member of the ancient Hebrew people who lived in Israel. Also refers to the Jews exiled and held in captivity in Babylonia in 597–538 B.C.E.

metaphors Figures of speech in which a term or phrase is used to represent something else

pastor A minister or leader in charge of a church

personification Giving human qualities to an animal, object, or idea

persuasion Convincing or urging someone to do something by appealing to reason

persuasive Intended to persuade

resistance To oppose, withstand, or strive against something

similes Figures of speech in which two things that are not alike are compared

Union The North, or free states in the American Civil War

Vietnam War A war in Vietnam from 1955 to 1975. The United States entered the war in 1955, first as advisors to France, who was an ally of South Vietnam, and later with troops

white supremacist A person who believes in racism and believes that white people are superior to other races

world wars Major wars fought between all or most countries of the world

INDEX

ABOUT THE AUTHOR

Rebecca Sjonger is the author of more than 50 nonfiction books for young people. American history is one of her favorite subjects to write about. She loves the challenge of separating facts from fiction while researching.